Sad Nan

by Gabriel Hernandez
illustrated by Luanne Marten

Practice Decodable 3

McGraw Hill Education

Bothell, WA • Chicago, IL • Columbus, OH • New York, NY

MHEonline.com

Send all inquiries to:
McGraw-Hill Education
8787 Orion Place
Columbus, OH 43240

ISBN: 978-0-02-144934-7
MHID: 0-02-144934-1

Printed in China.

9 10 11 12 13 DSS 27 26 25 24 23

I have a pal.

Sad, damp Nan.

Snap!

I have a plan.

Snap!

I am damp.

I am as sad as Nan.

Nan!